Daily Quotes from "Words of the Heart"

by Gerondissa Makrina Vassopoulou

Author/Compiler of Quotes:

Elizabeth P. Fitzgerald

Introduction:

"Asia Minor...This holy land was the birthplace of Gerondissa Makrina of blessed memory, foundress and abbess (1963 - 1995) of the Holy Monastery of Panagia Odigitria, Portaria, Volos, [Greece]. Born in the year 1921 to God-fearing parents, Photios and Anastasia Vassopoulos, Gerondissa's birth name was Maria Vassopoulou.

[W]hen she was seven year old, the Lord called her to the angelic life of monasticism.

Gerondissa Makrina was adorned with an abundance of virtues, which sprang forth from her Christ-centered life and her genuine ascetic conduct. She was especially distinguished for her warmhearted hospitality and charity.

Whenever the sisters made fresh homemade bread, it was Gerondissa Makrina's great joy to give it out as a blessing.

The day of Gerondissa's repose was the Sunday of the Holy Fathers of the First Ecumenical Council, June 4, 1995 (May 22 on the Old Calendar).

Notes:

Throughout this book, "The prayer" is the Jesus prayer, "Lord Jesus Christ, have mercy on me."

The "nous" is the eye of the soul.

"Theoria" can refer to either of two different states:

1) Spiritual contemplation of divine things initiated by man himself, or

2) A state of prayer in which the nous is taken up (enraptured) into heavenly realms and enlightened.

January

January 1st

Whether we are monastics or laypeople, we should have theoria, saying, "Let us now go for a walk through Paradise," even if we do not see Paradise. We must be very attentive to our thoughts, because God loves purity of the mind very much.

January 2nd

When a person prays and loves Christ immensely, his entire body is sanctified, and he exudes fragrance. Christ does not discriminate; anyone can achieve this.

January 3rd

The minutes and hours are passing. The days and years roll by. Everything passes by, and what is left to man is his obedience to the will of God.

January 4th

When a person has God in his soul and separates the good from the bad, removing what is bad from his soul, then he thinks that there are flowers everywhere.

January 5th

We must bind our nous, just as the soldiers bind their provision sacks. When the nous tries to leave, we will say, "Come here! Where do you think you're going? To criticize? To wander about? Sit here, vagabond."

January 6th

Strive to not stain the scroll where your deeds are recorded.

January 7th

The compassion of God is like a vast ocean. A soul is able to bear everything else: divine flame, love and eros, sweetness, etc. All things can be endured, but not this compassion. So great is His compassion. One calls out then, "I am not able to bear it!"

January 8th

Are we not human? We fall. However, we must get up. Christ loves us so much. Who loves us? He Who created the entire world.

January 9th

If we love [God], we will long for Him, as we would for someone dear to us.

January 10th

When I take my nous to Paradise, I find a multitude of companions. Who will I not find there? Angels, archangels, saints, and martyrs are all there. We are not alone. Christ will be within us when we cultivate the gifts of God in our soul.

January 11th

When a person's nous is in Heaven, he is interested in nothing else. Then he says, "O, that I had wings as a dove!" And other times he says, "Grant me years that I may serve Christ." Here and in Paradise, he sees everything as golden.

January 12th

Great patience is needed in our life because everyone has their passions and weaknesses. Therefore, let us say a prayer for the salvation of every soul that suffers and does not know how to live correctly, and thus, divine forbearance will come into our soul.

January 13th

The more steps one takes for God and the more one works for God, the more one will be repaid by God. ...Whatever we give, He accepts; nothing goes to waste.

January 14th

We must aspire to obtain a spiritual upbringing. Spiritual education is grandeur within a person. God will teach him how to sleep, how to get up, how to be careful of himself, how to behave all day.

January 15th

[An ascetic in the Kleisoura area of Castoria] said to me, "...When people come [to the monastery], you will tell them that just as they clean their houses - even in the nooks and crannies - and take out the garbage, that is how they should clean their souls. They have to make a sincere confession to remove everything and clean the house of their soul.

January 16th

Why is it that as soon as we leave the church, sleep departs, our eyes immediately open, and we begin talking, while at the hour of prayer when we should be talking with God, we are overcome by sleepiness and listlessness? Because the devil strives to hinder our soul from being united to God! Great attentiveness and fervent prayer are necessary so that the devil does not captivate our nous.

January 17th

Besides judging, we must be careful not to spread the words of others, especially regarding false accusations. Each person has his own inner world. As far as how each person lives, that is a matter of conscience. Sometimes the conscience becomes calloused and one does not realize it. ...But when a person is spiritual and prays unceasingly, entreating God, God...will open the eyes of his soul.

January 18th

When we go to pray, we must have nothing inside us against our neighbor, not even the slightest stain. In other words, we have to keep our mind spotless, without the tiniest blemish, so that grace will overshadow us, heavenly refreshment will visit us, and a heavenly flame will engulf us.

January 19th

If we cling to the fringe of the Panagia's garment, She will take us to Paradise. Let us cling to the fringe of Her garment and love Christ fervently: "Thou shalt love the Lord thy God with all thy heart, and with all thy soul, and with all thy mind..." What a beautiful thing, what majesty to love our God so much that our soul departs!

January 20th

My little soul, you gain nothing if you do not "love your God with all your soul, with all your mind, with all your strength, and your neighbor as yourself." We must learn to "judge not that ye be not judged." If we keep these two commandments, we will go all together to Christ; we will go to Paradise with great ease.

January 21st

The more one labors and sweats, the greater the reward he will receive, and the more God will embrace him. God will pay each of us, taking into account each person's strength and their spiritual and physical illnesses. God has so much love for us, so much compassion!

January 22nd

If Adam and Eve had been obedient, they would have remained in Paradise. They lost Paradise through disobedience.

January 23rd

We must strive to cultivate love. If we study the Gospel of Saint John the Theologian every day, it will benefit us greatly. We should have much love for Saint John the Theologian and cling to him. ...We should have great reverence for him, praying to him fervently to give us forbearance and help us reach divine dispassion.

January 24th

How beautiful it is for God to come into our soul!

January 25th

We must always make a new beginning because we will fall and fail in one thing or another. The word of God is so quickly expelled from the soul - we hear it now and then immediately forget it...

January 26th

God has richly given us His earthly and heavenly blessings. When I say heavenly blessings I mean that when a person has watchfulness and prayer, he can progress and ascend step by step.

January 27th

We should have wings on our soul, not paying attention to earthly things. Keep your eyes on your God. Worship Him. Put your heart in the nous of God so that God will keep you in His nous ceaselessly.

January 28th

Many people who partake of antidoron are overwhelmed with grace as if they received Holy Communion. The word "antidoron" means "instead of the Holy Gifts." We should receive antidoron and holy water with great piety. First we should venerate the icons, and then receive antidoron. ...We will make a bow and venerate the icons...

January 29th

Where is the love of Christ? I hunger and thirst for the love of God. Where can I find it? What can I do? How can I delight in it? We must compel ourselves. Let us sing a Paraklesis to the Panagia. Let us say, "Most Holy Theotokos, save us." Let us do all that is holy.

January 30th

[W]hen a person has faith and love for God, he is not afraid since "perfect love casteth out fear." Night is turned into day.

January 31st

The more often we can gather our mind on the magnificence of God, the more our soul will begin to perceive it little by little.

February

February 1st

If we gain all the goods of the whole world and harm our precious soul, we have lost everything. Therefore, we must do whatever is in our strength to do.

February 2nd

Prayer is the greatest gift of God, and when God's love overcomes a person, then when he prays he feels like he is being cleansed.

February 3rd

When people come to the monastery they say, "Oh! How beautiful! You have a piece of Paradise here." This is exactly how it is. ...God magnifies everything, and He makes the nous all light, all joy. The person sees even a flower as something magnificent.

February 4th

May God help us repent for our sins with compunction and contrition. This will happen when we pray and beseech Christ to enlighten us, so that we understand our mistakes.

February 5th

We must prepare ourselves for the Jerusalem on high. We should make use of our time now; otherwise, we will regret wasting our days since we do not know what is in the future and what will come to pass.

February 6th

At the hour of death a person sees before him every good deed he has ever done decorated with diamonds. ...The more one labors, the more grace he will receive.

February 7th

Whoever humbles himself more and asks forgiveness will find more divine grace.

February 8th

When joyful mourning comes, humility will also appear, and then a person says, "O, that I had wings as a dove," and at other times, he will say, "My God, give me years that I may labor for You."

February 9th

[I]t takes spiritual forcefulness and a little labor in order to find this pearl [the prayer], which is all sweetness, light, fire, and refreshment. Joy to the one who compels himself to discover this majesty!

February 10th

Let us avoid the devil's traps and look only to ourselves. Where did we sadden God? Did we please Him? Only then will we make progress without straying from our goal.

February 11th

For a single glass of cool water that we give someone, we receive back a hundredfold. If we read and study the Gospel, keeping and putting it into practice, we will fly with wings to get some water or a treat when we see someone coming.

February 12th

[W]hen one has a spiritual education, he will be attentive with everything - the services, prostrations, etc. He will struggle, weep, do his prayer rule, read the Holy Scriptures, kneel in prayer, and in this way, he will receive the grace of God. Without the grace of God, a person cannot progress.

February 13th

One Divine Liturgy is worth more than a billion dollars. One may practice a multitude of virtues, but nothing compares to the Mystery. Divine Liturgy is the Divine Sacrifice. When the Sacrifice takes place, the priest says silently, "Remember, O Lord, the living and the dead...," and at that time we can commemorate the names of the living and the dead. At that moment, earth and Heaven are united and miracles happen.

February 14th

We have said at other times that when there is verbal judging, there is also inward judging. Many times verbal judging harms everyone. Inward judging harms the very person who judges, but this is the greater sin.

February 15th

[W]hen there is even the slightest thing in the soul against one's brother - even something small, as small as a fly or a fly's wing or even the smallest insect - then prayer cannot progress.

February 16th

[The Fathers] prayed that this Gospel message would be imprinted on their souls so that they could live it. We live our lives carelessly. The good years pass; the good days pass; our good minutes slip by - even those slip between our fingers. The devil steals them from us and mocks us. He takes these beautiful days from us, this beautiful grandeur. He steals Paradise from us.

February 17th

If an employer pays extra to the one who works overtime, then won't God repay you when, for His love, you deprive yourself of going out or doing things you like to do? Is God unjust? No, He will repay you and bestow gifts upon you.

February 18th

If there is humility, there will be fear of God. If there is fear of God, the grace of God will come. If grace comes, one reaches repentance and reaches Heaven.

February 19th

St. John [the Theologian]'s nous was entirely light; just as light cannot be touched, that is how his nous was. We should love him and implore him because he continually spoke about love, "Little children, let us not love in words or in tongue, but in deed and truth." How beautiful!

February 20th

If a person does not hear the word of God, he cannot stand. Let us struggle as much as possible to be careful of our thoughts, to keep them on God and not let them wander.

February 21st

Do you see how the little lights down in Volos shine so brightly here and there? This is how the souls will be in Paradise. Some will shine more, some less, some faintly red.

February 22nd

A person who praises God is like the many-eyed cherubim. A person becomes many-eyed and runs to work like the cherubim, which fly continually, praising God: "Holy, Holy, Holy...." The many-eyed cherubim and six-winged seraphim do the will of God in the blink of an eye. With only a nod, in one second His will is carried out.

February 23rd

We should pay attention when venerating the icons, to venerate the feet of Christ and the hands of the Theotokos. It is not permissible to kiss the face of Christ or the Theotokos. Let us be attentive to this. Otherwise, we become bold, which is not proper for a monastic or anyone else.

February 24th

[S]ay a few words to our Panagia and to our Christ - communicate with Him - so He will come into your heart. This is what God wants from us. If we do this, we will experience so much grace in our souls that nothing else will matter to us. Our nous will be captivated by the love of God and the eros of Christ, and we will not be concerned about anything.

February 25th

If we do even one extra knot on our prayer rope, our guardian angel will record it; a few prayers or good thoughts will be stored up for later. Christ saves up all these things, and when the time comes for us to depart for the next life, we will take them and go to Christ.

February 26th

If one thinks of how much one has saddened God from his birth up to the present, both "in knowledge and in ignorance," he will then say, "Just as You, my Christ, bear with me and with the entire world, likewise I will also bear with my brother.

February 27th

Just think of the worm that never sleeps! Think of the eternal fire! When a person remembers Hell, he never sins. It makes the one who is quick to anger become meek. The passions subside, and the soul softens; it becomes tender like those little flowers that spring up and have so much freshness.

February 28th

These days, we should at least draw closer to the Holy Fathers with our intentions; we cannot match their works or their labors, sweat, and tears.

February 29th

We must attend to the matter of our salvation and not be superficial about it. Just as the ocean and the sky are endless, so much more endless is the compassion of God. Now He tolerates and puts up with us, but divine justice will come with glory. With fear and trembling the angels' trumpets will sound. What account will we give then?

March

March 1st

When we truly love Christ, we will cling to His neck; we will embrace His feet.

March 2nd

When someone has prayer, the All-Holy Spirit works inside his soul, and he finds himself in the Holy Spirit.

March 3rd

We say with pain, "My Christ, resurrect our hearts just as You resurrected Lazarus. In the same way, resurrect our own souls."

March 4th

God does not want cleverness. He wants only for you to worship Him and to keep Him noetically close by you. God gives spiritual intelligence and discernment to the person who is noetically close to Him.

March 5th

He who continually thinks about heavenly things has great joy and delight and tastes God. When he does not think about these things, he is pulled by earthly things that do not have any value.

March 6th

The more we please the unblemished eye of God, so much more will divine grace operate in our souls.

March 7th

If we knew what we lose every second, we would not be looking either right or left. Instead, all of our being, all of our speech during the entire day, would be directed towards God.

March 8th

In order for someone to conquer his passions, he must look only at himself, and not right or left. We must anticipate the passions and weaknesses that sprout up in our soul because if they grow strong, we will not be able to uproot them easily.

March 9th

When we ceaselessly pursue the prayer, God will enrich us. Only the prayer cleanses the heart.

March 10th

Let us pursue prayer. It will become a precious treasure in our soul. We will acquire heavenly experiences. We will be able to see Paradise everywhere.

March 11th

Let us make our nous an open book and reflect on death, Hades, and Paradise! We must grasp with our minds that after our death is God's judgment - in other words, where we will go and where we will stand, either in Hades or in Paradise.

March 12th

[T]he world has so much need of prayer that it is beyond words! If we only knew how much the saints run night and day to help us! Do we help others by praying for them? Do we commemorate names? Do we strive to be united with God in order to benefit the souls of others?

March 13th

Shouldn't we take into account the unblemished eye of God that sees everything? Has someone fallen? Let us pray, beseeching the Panagia for his repentance.

March 14th

Let us be very careful. ...anger, harsh words, idle talk, and grumbling...harm our soul. May your nous be Heaven, your heart the throne of God, and your mouth a church.

March 15th

When God commanded Moses to strike the rock (we saw the rock when we went to the Holy Land), he contradicted God within himself, saying, "Can water come out of this rock?" He heard a voice from the Lord telling him that for his contradiction, he would be deprived of the Promised Land. For talking back in his mind, he lost the Promised Land!

March 16th

We must ask God to give our soul watchfulness, to open the eyes of our soul and give us illumination to discern everything about ourselves.

March 17th

[In Church, when our nous is concentrated on the service]...the nous ascends to Heaven and feels the majesty of God. How beautiful it is to have a pure nous and experience that majesty, to see nothing in one's soul, except God alone! We must continually see the face of God noetically before us. Then we will neither desert nor slip away from the word of God.

March 18th

Was there an exchange of words, and we saddened someone? Immediately, "Forgive me. I saddened you. It's my fault. I have sinned." We should ask forgiveness with genuine love.

March 19th

If an employer is conscientious and takes care to reward your meticulous work, the efforts you make, and the time you sacrifice, then how much more will God repay you! We must make the resolution and say, "I will speak a few words to my Christ. I will communicate with Him."

March 20th

One time, I asked Geronda, and he told me that inner criticism is the most deadly sin. You judge without showing it on the outside; you seem to be all right, but inside you are full of thoughts. The soul of a person who judges inwardly is hardened like a rock, like the uncultivated ground, like an unfruitful field where nothing grows. He has two sins: judgmental thoughts and pride. In other words, out of egotism, he does not show that he judged.

March 21st

Where there is love, a person can bear everything - sorrows and worries, temptations and thoughts, even various tragic events like wars, earthquakes, disasters, etc. This is how much grace helps him.

March 22nd

Let us entreat our Christ to give us awareness and humility. Let us not take ourselves into account; we should always be the last of all. ...We have nothing good, absolutely nothing, since everything is a gift of God.

March 23rd

We should take up our prayer rope and pray to help those who are ill. With one little prayer rope that we do, a sick man can be healed, or a soul that is in sin can be illumined.

March 24th

A good word benefits a person, calms him immediately, and his conscience is at peace because he did not harm or sadden anyone. This is how the Fathers worked and maintained the grace of God in their souls. Bitter words should be expelled. When they come to you, bite your tongue, even to the point of drawing blood, so that you do not sadden your brother.

March 25th

The Samaritan woman had good intentions, and for this she was made worthy to see Christ. She had good intentions but had not found anyone to guide her. She then found Christ Himself, Who waited for her at the well, and she asked for the living water.

March 26th

We have said that there are more angels in the church than the breaths we take. At that hour, there are holy angels and archangels present, but our eyes - mine, first of all - cannot see anything because they are heavy with sleep, blinded by laziness and forgetfulness. However, those who are pious pay attention to the words being said, and their mind is on the prayer. Thus, their spirit leaves and is caught up in theoria, and they experience heavenly things.

March 27th

Oh, how God makes a person heavenly, if only they want it!

March 28th

[W]hen our Geronda was a young boy, I would see him daily. When he wanted silence so he could focus on noetic prayer, he would leave his house and come to mine. He stayed in a room and did his prayers there. I locked the door and left. Sometimes I would go to work and sometimes to the store to shop. When I returned I would find the floor flooded with the tears he shed in his prayers.

March 29th

The hour of death is very difficult. At that hour, the angels run to take the soul, the demons also run with their manuscripts, and a battle takes place. Our guardian angel appears with his manuscript, saying, "This soul has confessed, it has these virtues, it has this, it has that."

March 30th

[W]hen something bothers you in your thoughts, do not dwell on it, but rather, throw it out immediately.

When we do not stop the thoughts in time, a wall is erected and it blocks the Sun from rising and divine grace does not shine in our souls.

March 31st

Every morning when we get up, we should immediately put on our iron helmet and the breastplate and our iron boots so we can confront the devil in whatever way he will attack us. ...Breastplate? It is prayer, which protects and watches over us so that we follow the will of God. The iron boots? They allow us to walk safely through the thorns and rocks. What is the helmet? Humility.

April

April 1st

If there is something troubling our soul, and as human beings we fall, we should say, "Help me, my Christ; strengthen me; enlighten me; bestow more faith upon me, more love; grant me obedience." The soul will seek after these things because it desires salvation.

April 2nd

When we acquire prayer, it will be a light and a guardian in our soul because God will protect us and will not abandon us.

April 3rd

We should never make excuses for ourselves, saying what we did was right. Let us beseech God to enlighten us, so that with a pure nous we may see our own faults.

April 4th

If a day goes by and one does not enjoy and feel God's presence, the day is wasted; everything else is worthless.

April 5th

When we have humility, God will make His dwelling within us. We will be at rest, and wherever we are, we will see everything as heavenly.

April 6th

I do not allow a bad thought about you to stay with me even for a second, because I know that this becomes an obstacle for Christ to come into our souls.

April 7th

Every passion that sprouts up needs to be cut down. Much humility is needed for us to progress in the grandeur of God's love.

April 8th

Because we are full of passions, we should sympathize with one another and be careful of our tongue. "The tongue has no bones, but it crushes bones." If we use it for God, it will be all honey and sweetness. If we say words against each other, it will be all bitterness.

April 9th

Let us do everything with the fear of God and abundant love.

April 10th

May you be worthy to become dwellings and chosen vessels of the All-Holy-Spirit.

April 11th

We are nothing, but let us sympathize with those in pain, and let us pray for them so we can help them and thus do the will of God.

April 12th

What can I say? I worked among two thousand people, and I tried to hold on to what was needful. I was not interested in what anyone else was doing. A thousand things went on beside me, and I paid no attention. I said the prayer continually and nothing else.

April 13th

Let us keep the Gospel commandment that says, "Judge not, that ye be not judged." Whoever keeps this commandment of the Gospel will go to God without judgment.

April 14th

How many times do we judge and criticize and put ourselves above everyone else? When we think, "I am better; there is no one like me," this does the greatest harm to our soul. This is inner, secret pride. If we don't humble ourselves...and if we don't say to ourselves, "How can I insult or judge or say things about others?" the grace of God cannot visit our souls.

April 15th

Whoever feels the compassion of God is unable to say a word about anyone else. ...[I]f someone does something to him, he'll excuse him, saying, "He didn't mean to do that to me." The saints always have this kind of reserve and make excuses for everyone.

April 16th

The spiritual struggle has great depth and height; it is difficult, but it has the grace of God. Whoever struggles will perceive God in his soul. He will see the majesty of God and say, "My Christ, You came to me? To me, the unclean vessel?"

April 17th

Do you have resentment? Chase away the thoughts. Good conduct drives the snake out of the hole.

April 18th

The palace guard stands at attention for hours, without moving his gaze, without moving his hands, feet, or anything else. If we have such forcefulness with ourselves in prayer, God will grant spiritual things to our soul that one cannot comprehend, that cannot be described with our earthen tongue. This grandeur of God cannot be described.

April 19th

The saints help us when we read their lives attentively, and then we have their blessing.

April 20th

The important thing is to try to have an illumined nous, not to accept unclean notions or anything else inside us - judging, anger, wrath, wandering thoughts, and various bad thoughts that fight us and drag us to and fro. Just like when we clean fruit and throw away anything bad and rotten because the house will fill with flies and stink...

April 21st

Humility! When we humble ourselves, will we say things about others? We will not say anything at all! ...What can we say about others when our own passions and shortcomings are like a camel's hump?

April 22nd

Who knows if God will help some person from the one little prayer rope that we do? We will have consolation and joy within ourselves. You can offer as much charity as you want with your prayer rope.

April 23rd

We should think of how to draw closer to the love of God, how to raise our minds to God, our Creator, and to the heavenly beauty of Paradise. How lovely! What delight!

April 24th

We should focus on how to please God and what words to speak to Him. Our Christ wants us to talk to Him, not just to say a dry "Lord Jesus Christ, have mercy on me." He wants us to speak to Him so He can save us.

April 25th

[In Church] When you make an effort to stay in one place and stand still, you will comprehend much more. Abundant grace will overshadow your souls because this is self-denial and forcing yourself; in that hour, you are striving to do something for God.

April 26th

We were young then. ...We walked an hour each night to attend the Forty-Day Liturgies served by the older Fr. Ephraim. We did not take anything into account, not even snow, rain, or wind. ...[W]e put a little blanket on our heads, and we went in the middle of the night.

April 27th

If we are careful to decorate our house with gold and velvet and the best we have when we are expecting an important guest, how much more should we take care when we want to receive Holy Communion? How should we approach the Holy Mysteries to receive our Christ?

April 28th

The infinite compassion of God visits a holy man, and he thinks of the immense ocean of God's love that is endless. "Thou shalt love thy neighbor as thyself." Think of it. What an awesome thing this love is; a person murders, he fornicates, and yet you love him!

April 29th

We should not hold anything negative inside us, not even a trace. We should show love and forgiveness to everyone as much as possible.

April 30th

Being judgmental has many dangerous traps that are unimaginable, including idle talk, mockery, laughter, yelling, lying, and many other sins. All the great and deadly sins begin from judging.

May

May 1st

The Holy Spirit refreshes like a breeze or the morning dew. Sometimes He approaches like a flame, and you say, "Where is this fire coming from?" or like a breath of air, and you look around to see from where it originates, but you see nothing. These kinds of spiritual experiences occur within the soul. Sometimes you think that you are in the middle of glowing embers, yet you are not burning. This flame consumes your insides and your heart and fills your nous with light. But it does not burn; instead it refreshes.

May 2nd

We need to diligently avoid idle talk because idle talk is like a wildfire, as the Holy Fathers say. Just as we have seen entire forests burned down in Penteli and in Kiphisia, and their hills left bare, in the same way idle talk removes every good thing from inside our souls.

May 3rd

If one prays and his nous is united with God, he receives so much joy! ...He prays as he feels: sometimes with his hands raise up, sometimes like a convict with his hands crossed and his eyes flooded with tears, and sometimes kneeling like he is at the feet of Christ. This comes in a spiritual way, not in one's imagination.

May 4th

A day should not escape us without spiritual communication with God, because this communication makes one holy, a god by grace. You should pursue the prayer fervently like those who search for a pearl.

May 5th

The power of Christ is immeasurably greater than the power of the devil.

May 6th

We have a lot of egotism and hidden conceit; this is why we cannot handle even one comment and we immediately react.

May 7th

We need to protect our eyes and our ears and ceaselessly pray in order to have the grace of God. The more we struggle, the more we will set aside spiritual reserves, and we will not fear anything, no matter what comes.

May 8th

I saw many walls and when the sun had risen a little, only a few rays of light passed through between them. Then I heard a voice say to me that this is how it is for the person who does not do the works of God as he should.

May 9th

The grace of the Holy Spirit is within us and can be operating in us even if we do not understand it; the prayer is doing its work. "Lord Jesus Christ, have mercy on me." - we say the prayer, and at some point God will overshadow us.

May 10th

Since everyone wants love, and since we seek to be respected and to be spoken to with love, we should behave likewise towards others.

May 11th

The Holy Fathers had great charity, and they prayed with immense faith. They had such love and eros for Christ, such gratitude, that they considered the greens they ate to be a wonderful gift and the cave they lived in to be a blessing, a very great blessing. God rewarded them with great joy, progress, and delight.

May 12th

Instead of making excuses, it is better to look after our souls, to think how we have behaved during the day, to see our falls and our unworthiness.

May 13th

Whatever you do for God, you receive back a hundredfold. God will not abandon us; He repays us for everything. Let us avoid all evil and look only at ourselves, and we will find that no one else is at fault.

May 14th

Of course, we will fall at some point in our struggle. However, we should say, "I fell…I made this mistake. The demons defeated me in this; I am fought by that. The devil threw me into this, into remembrance of wrongs, anger, wrath, internal judging, pride." Then we will see how the grace of God will work in us.

May 15th

[T]he person who has felt the compassion of God will hold his tongue and be careful not to criticize another. When he listens to his conscience, he won't censure others. His conscience holds him back, and in this way his life passes pleasantly, and he is joyful. How beautiful is unity! How beautiful are love, good behavior, and courtesy.

May 16th

Let us be very…attentive during the Divine Liturgy. The Divine Liturgy is priceless! It works countless miracles! We must have love for God, love for our neighbor, love for the entire world.

May 17th

Let us think of the majesty of God and what He has prepared for us in Heaven! God has prepared everything for us in Heaven. His love is boundless. He has so much love for us that no matter how many times we fall, His embrace is still open.

May 18th

[A priest I met in Athens before the war] was a very holy man who has passed away now. He related to me how he saw the Holy Mystery, the cherubim and the seraphim. When he would say, "…the many-eyed cherubim and six-winged seraphim…," his mind left the earth, his nous transcended earthly things, and he felt immense grace in his soul. Oh, how God transforms man, how He sustains him, maintains him, and gives him life!

May 19th

Is it possible that God will not break that stony heart of ours to pieces, bending it and pushing aside the boulders that we do not even realize exist inside it? That is how it is! That is God's love and boundless compassion. This is why the Fathers said, "O Lord, cease the waves of Your grace," because they were given so much grace that they could not endure the compassion of God.

May 20th

Every day, let us make our mind Heaven, our heart the throne of God and our mouth a church.

May 21st

Once when I was kneeling during the Cherubic Hymn, I saw [the Panagia] as a fifteen-year-old little girl, just as She looks in the icon "Quick to Hear," which I have in my cell. She was standing before the Royal Doors with the Christ Child in Her arms. I will never forget Her sweet eyes and how they looked at me. Her gaze penetrated my heart. ...[T]he Panagia smiled at me, filling me with serenity by Her gaze and from that moment lifting my spirits.

May 22nd

Let us take care to listen to our conscience and to set it at ease. The matter of our conscience is essential. When one obeys his conscience, he is full of joy and delight, and he sleeps worry-free.

May 23rd

What will take place in Heaven! The souls will meet and keep company, enjoying heavenly blessings and walking among flowers and verdure. What joy and delight there will be! Everywhere they will praise God.

May 24th

If a person is continually in a state of prayer, he beholds a light in his soul, a splendor, a majesty. An abundance of consoling tears come to him, so sweet that nothing earthly compares. He feels a satiety that the mind cannot comprehend.

May 25th

The saints whose lives we read will intercede for us when we give them our attention. We will be astonished by their lives, we will be moved, we will mourn, we will be filled with devotion, we will honor them and make them our own, and we will say, "O Holy Saint of God, intercede for us."

May 26th

We walked for an hour, at three in the morning, to attend the Divine Liturgy and receive Holy Communion. We would say the Jesus prayer, "Lord Jesus Christ, have mercy on us," while Fr. Ephraim did the Holy Proskomidi. We would hear him say, "Thou didst ransom us...." Then Fr. Ephraim would call out, "One of the soldiers pierced His side with a spear and immediately blood and water came out." What an experience that was! What tears of compunction we all shed! There was complete silence ...we heard him say all the mystical prayers aloud. It was majestic!

May 27th

The compassion of God is an abyss; it is unfathomable. Man's intellect cannot comprehend it. The Fathers that experienced the magnificence of God were able to receive all of His gifts.

May 28th

Surely we are not perfect; we are human beings. A judgmental thought will pass through your mind, but do not allow it to remain and take root until it becomes almost impossible to remove.

May 29th

We should have love: "Thou shalt love the Lord thy God with all thy heart, and with all thy soul, and with all thy mind, and thy neighbor as thyself." These are the words of Christ! How beautiful! We should love God above all and our neighbor as ourselves. The grace of God will strengthen us when we have this great love.

May 30th

We need to remember God! When we think of someone we love, our mind is filled with delight and our heart is filled even more. How much more then should we feel delight when we think of God and the Panagia!

May 31st

As long as one humbles himself, he sees the infinite magnitude of God's compassion. He gazes upon the sky and the sea and deepens his understanding of the infinite compassion of God.

June

June 1st

When God sees our pain and tears, He will help us. When we understand that some evil is gaining a victory over us, whether it be anger, curiosity, negligence, gloom, or insensitivity, we must beg and beseech our God.

June 2nd

When a soul is humbled, it begins to feel compassion, love, and reverence, and it does not accept judgmental thoughts. In perceiving this great affection, this great love of Christ, you overlook whatever fault you see in another, saying, "Oh, but Christ has shown me so much love, so much affection. ...how can I show myself ungrateful?"

June 3rd

Did you sadden someone created in the image and likeness of God? Immediately humble yourself. Why should we feel sorry for ourselves? We are dust and ashes. This is the way the Fathers battled and conquered their passions.

June 4th

Whoever pursues the prayer as if it were gold and makes use of every minute is able to leap over all obstacles, accepting and enduring everything. Then,

God and the Panagia protect this person. He will be careful not to judge…

June 5th

You should not get angry when you are scolded, nor should you love to be praised, but rather desire to be humbled.

June 6th

When a small child calls out, "I want bread! I am hungry," does his mother not run and prepare him something to eat? Likewise, if all day we call out, "We want to be saved! We want to be saved! Lord Jesus Christ, have mercy on us," will Christ not send us His mercy? It is impossible for this not to happen.

June 7th

When a person prays, he sees from where the devil is coming to attack him, but when he is careless, negligent, and hardhearted, the demons sneak up on him, creating commotion…. Our nous needs to be vigilant, ceaselessly saying the name of Christ.

June 8th

"How awesome God is! Despite the fact that we sin and put up obstacles which impede us, still a little light comes and tries to warm us and revive us, and in this way we have a little consolation from time to time."

June 9th

The name of God operates in our soul in the same manner that fortifying medicines and hearty foods strengthen our body.

June 10th

We have to confront the devil who will make a display of our sins before angels and archangels. Right now we take this superficially, but if the hour of death comes and we are ascending the ladder, then we will tremble.

June 11th

Oh, how God adorned the Holy Fathers of old with light, and made them able to see the beauty of Paradise and those sweet-smelling blossoms of the divine Word! They beheld them and strove harder. The more they beheld, the more they struggled.

June 12th

What is the outcome when a sister keeps her mind on God? She observes her own actions and why she behaved as she did, and realizes when she has misunderstood something. She thinks, "My sister is human; she fell today, and tomorrow I will fall."

June 13th

The greatest beast is our own self. If we fight ourselves, every evil thing will depart from us.

June 14th

When the grace of God visits a person, a heavenly, incomprehensible Light comes into his soul.

June 15th

Every disorderly movement in church distracts the mind of the one praying.

June 16th

Remember what Sister Agapia said, "May the entire world be saved, the entire world." God has given her an abundance of love.

June 17th

We should say to our soul, "Come let's go to the beauties of Paradise! We should have this theoria. If it is so beautiful here, if here the flowers are so fragrant, if this place is like a piece of Paradise, just think of the beauty of Paradise!

June 18th

One time I went to a home where I met some people who asked me the following question... "If someone finds himself at a table where there is good fruit and not-so-good fruit, which should he prefer, the good or the bad? Is it a sin to eat the good fruit?" "When he has self-denial, he'll eat the bad fruit and not the good."

June 19th

My God, help me; give me Your forbearance; give me Your love. Grant me to love everyone, whatever they may do and whatever may happen, even something bad. Give me the proper love, so I can love others the way You love Your Son.

June 20th

We see the vast sea, the infinite sky; thus is the compassion of God, thus is the love of God, and likewise this is how our mind must become! …let us reflect on the compassion of God.

June 21st

Love is the greatest virtue. "Thou shalt love the Lord thy God with all thy soul, with all thy mind, and thy neighbor as thyself." When we hold this commandment tightly in our hand and reflect on it every day, it will help us immeasurably as the first and foremost commandment.

June 22nd

I remember one stationmaster who told me, "Gerondissa, I try to put my conscience at ease so that I sleep light and peacefully." It made an impression on me how a layperson struggles to appease his conscience. What a beautiful thing for one to have a peaceful conscience that does not convict him of anything!

June 23rd

The days roll by and worldly things occupy us. God is a righteous wage-giver, and He records and repays whoever toils. He counts their footsteps, their labors, their effort, their weeping, their tears and sighs, their vigil; He records everything.

June 24th

[Our Christ] invites us continually so that He can bestow His gifts upon us. If we were to see what He has prepared for us in Heaven, we would be in awe. The beauty of Paradise cannot be conceived by the human mind. It is awesome, it is tremendous, it is so beautiful, and the soul feels such an abundance of delight! We need to have love; we must love God. If we love Him, He will freely give us everything. We only have to give Him our heart.

June 25th

If I am in debt to a certain store, I will not be able to easily pass by there because my conscience will convict me. In the same way we should not leave our debt unpaid to the true God. We do not even know if we will live until night or wake up in the morning.

June 26th

When you do not owe the store owner and you pass by, he will call out to you, "Come in, what would you like me to give you? This is what Christ does, "Come, what would you like? Do you want honey? Do you want grace? Take from here, take from there," and He grants us everything. Christ bestows gifts on us; He provides us with every gift.

June 27th

When a person is captivated in prayer, he becomes longsuffering, meek, abstinent, and humble.

June 28th

We must struggle to be spiritual people, bearers of the Holy Spirit. Prayer reaches the Holy Trinity. This is why people ask for things in prayer; this is why miracles happen. The sick are made well, sinners repent, and those led astray are illumined and return to the right path.

June 29th

Let us make a good beginning so that God may grant us repentance, because the person who has repentance does not have pride or egotism. May God grant us awareness of ourselves so that we may have humility.

June 30th

You see, the holy angels have ranks, and they each have different garments. Some angels' wings are gold; other angels have wings of light; others' wings are green, some blue, others red - all in different shades of color. One's eyes cannot get enough of the magnificence of the wings of the angels in Heaven! What takes place in Heaven is ineffable!

July

July 1st

…won't our Christ listen to us? He will say, "My child is praying and beseeching Me. …I will help him because he is calling on Me."

July 2nd

…did we sadden Christ? Let us say, "Forgive me!"

July 3rd

Just as we are continually eating in order to maintain the body, so the soul should constantly be fed with prayer. The one who prays ceaselessly feels divine blessedness and has the help of God.

July 4th

Humility is needed. When one looks to himself, he will see everything around him with a good eye. When a person has God within his soul, he does not speak ill of anyone, and when he sees someone who is suffering, he feels pain, weeps with him, and entreats God to be merciful to him.

July 5th

We are not alone. Look how many saints we have close to us! They come as soon as we call on them, but we do not call on then, and that is why we feel loneliness.

July 6th

When we are continuously saying the prayer at our work, we will be approaching God, and we will begin to know ourselves.

July 7th

The demon of pride and egotism battles all people today. If we do not throw off these passions, we will not see God within us. In the Gospel, Christ says that for even one idle word we will give an account to God.

July 8th

…our salvation is essential, and we should not take it lightly or consider it a shallow matter. We must add a little fear of God and a little self-denial to our struggle… We must pursue the name of God.

July 9th

If God hears the prayer, "Lord Jesus Christ, have mercy on me," He will keep us under His protection. He will guard us and will not let the evil one touch us.

July 10th

Oh, how carefully we should conduct our lives, not only we in the monastic life, but the laypeople in the world as well! Therefore, we must have a little fear of God in our soul.

July 11th

We do not have anything - neither physical nor spiritual strength. We are fought by illness, we are fought by the passions, we are fought by everything, and we cannot reach God... Through good intentions, a person becomes an ascetic... Through good intentions, one can become a martyr. Let us at least keep these things in mind so God can see that we are making an effort.

July 12th

Do we have a temptation? Let us remember how the martyrs were thrown to the lions! As for us, no one has severed even one piece of our flesh.... Let us be patient. It is a temptation, and it will pass.

July 13th

When the grace of God visits us, we see nothing wrong. When the grace of God leaves, we see and criticize everything; we notice even the slightest detail.

July 14th

Let us struggle to have humility in our soul. Humility! Whoever humbles himself and becomes "dust and ashes," is the one who will receive the majesty of God. He will receive the gifts of the All-Holy Spirit in his soul.

July 15th

Can an insect or anything else approach a light? No!
It will be burned! The insects stand far off and see the
light without approaching it. This is what happens
when the Light of grace dwells in a person's soul; the
passions stand far away.

July 16th

We should not speak harshly, but meekly, because
harshness obstructs the grace of God.

July 17th

Christ is a generous wage-giver; He is not unfair to us.
Are we careful of our mind? He repays us. Are we
careful of our heart? He gives to us. Are we careful of
our mouth? He rewards us. For whatever our feet do,
whatever our hands do, whatever our minds do, our
eyes, our ears, God will give us a reward. If we guard
our five senses, our Christ will have mercy on us and
fill us with grace.

July 18th

We must be attentive not to let a sinful condition linger
and become a passion in our soul. As soon as we say
something improper, let us immediately say, "Forgive

me," and be very watchful so that our soul does not become coarse.

July 19th

This wall is in front of the one who judges, blocking the light. The light shines on each one of the faithful. However, when there are judgmental thoughts, there is an obstruction, and although you see a ray of light here and there, the wall won't allow you to see God clearly. When we get up in the morning and pray to God without allowing any stain to remain in our soul, and we fight to keep our thoughts from being polluted, then we keep our nous pure.

July 20th

God is entirely love. "Love bears all things, believes all things, hopes all things, endures all things." Love achieves everything. When there is no love, then our bad thoughts persist and will not leave. We push Christ aside, even though He has His arms wide open, saying, "Come, My child. Come, My little child. Come, My dear. Come, My diamond. Where can I put you? Come into My embrace.

July 21st

This is why the Gospel tells us to forgive seventy times seven, because the passions weigh all of us down. This is why we must also bear with one another. We are given a sack to carry that is very heavy, and little by little we lift it.

July 22nd

"Love one another," and "God is love." Saint John the Theologian showed us that with love, we draw closer to God. As we know, he had great love for and faith in Christ, and so Christ loved him and entrusted His Mother to him.

July 23rd

Just as when we try to sift flour in a silk sifter and nothing passes through, in exactly the same way we have to sift our thoughts so that nothing bad passes through and so that our thoughts remain clean, undefiled, entirely chaste, and full of gladness, delight, and joy. Then grace unites us to God, making us one.

July 24th

Prayer is the greatest gift to man. Whoever cultivates prayer will delight in it and will feel the fragrant blossoms, the sweetness, and the honey of grace. He will be worthy to become one with God, to have theosis in his soul, and to become a god by grace.

July 25th

The evil one fears prayer like nothing else. However, he is happy to see sluggishness and sloth.

July 26th

It is a great gift for someone to please God. When you are careful, God will give you benefits. He will increase your wages. Did you work for one hour? He will pay you for two. God pays generously.

July 27th

When one pursues prayer, he delights in the rich magnificence of divine grace.

July 28th

A sick person in the hospital is healed, and we wonder how they were made well. They were healed from the prayers of the monastics and faithful.

July 29th

I pray that all together we may reach the Jerusalem on high and rejoice there, where there is beauty, love, delight, the majesty of God, and the fragrant flowers of Paradise, which are all equal in height - so beautiful and delightful that it is indescribable!

July 30th

Oh, how the devil keeps us occupied with all the earthly things here, and deprives us of the splendor in Heaven! You see the angels' garments some red, some blue, some yellow - garments made of gold and diamonds! The saints are ranked in order....

July 31st

We should never ask, "Why?" We should say, "This is what God allowed. Not one hair of my head falls without the will of God." It is very important that we keep this in mind. It is something heavenly.

August

August 1st

Our Lord gives us every opportunity to be saved, but if we do not choose to comprehend this, we have only ourselves to blame.

August 2nd

Think about where Christ went and what He did. Where was He? He was in Bethany were Martha and Mary lived who loved Him so greatly. Their brother got sick and they informed Jesus, their Teacher. Then they waited with anxiety, with tears, with pain, for the Master Christ to raise up their brother. So it is now for us who are awaiting the resurrection of our souls.

August 3rd

Our passions are so alive and so strong that in an instant we lose control of ourselves, because we do not pursue prayer.

August 4th

Through prayer, we will heal our brother's wound and overcome every difficult situation. When a person understands that he is a zero, he neither gets angry, nor speaks unkindly, nor argues, but instead he prays for others.

August 5th

The more we call on Christ, the more He approaches us and gives us grace.

August 6th

The gifts of the Holy Spirit are love, joy, peace, faith, meekness, self-control, fear of God, patience, humility, guilelessness, zeal, goodness, self-denial, and divine eros. We should continually ponder these things and examine ourselves to see if we have them.

August 7th

Our carelessness is the reason we do not have divine grace and why everything goes wrong for us. We must remember our guardian angel. When we disdain him with our works, he is saddened and distances himself from us. But if all day long we keep in mind not to sadden our angel, he will have his wings open and will cover us.

August 8th

When we feel that our guardian angel is protecting and guarding us all day long, we will have much prayer and reverence. What an awesome thing it is to be attentive to the guardian of our soul!

August 9th

The entire foundation of our life is humility.

August 10th

The many-eyed cherubim are in the service of God; they stand at the feet of Christ, and they encircle His throne, ready at any moment to perform His will. God commands them by motioning to them without speaking. These are spiritual things, and to describe them exactly as the soul perceives them is impossible.

August 11th

We should say, "Did I keep God's commandments today? What did I keep? Love? Was I careful not to judge anyone? What did I add to my account? Prayer? Remembrance of God? No, nothing. Was I charitable? Did I pray for anyone? Not at all.

August 12th

Through humility, our Christ was crucified; everything was achieved through humility. Our Christ wants fervent love and immense faith. When we love Him,

He will also love us. He will have compassion for us, have mercy on us, and save us.

August 13th

The patience that you practice by standing in your place without unnecessary movement [during prayer] will be counted by God as a struggle, and He will reward you.

August 14th

...say, "If I do this, I will grieve my angel." We should have great love for the guardian angel of our soul so that he protects us from the envy of the devil.

August 15th

Fr. Ignatius, who is in Jerusalem, said, "Your monastery is a very holy place. The ground there is sanctified." Certainly, I have observed this myself. Many times, the grace of our Panagia appears here, and many people see Her.

August 16th

God upholds us as a favor to Her [the Panagia], and we should beseech Her on our knees for the whole world and for ourselves so that She will help us and free us from our passions and shortcomings.

August 17th

We are careful that we do not get sick or tired, and we eat, sleep, and make ourselves comfortable. If we love ourselves this much, how much more must we love our Christ? If we love Him, He will help us in our spiritual life. The more one struggles, the more progress one makes.

August 18th

Whoever is able to struggle in secret, without expecting to be repaid here, will receive heavenly rewards. We know what Saint Nektarios did. He would get up at night and do a multitude of tasks at the Rizario Academy, even getting up to do the janitor's job when the janitor was sick. What will we offer to God?

August 19th

Coarseness obstructs the grace of God, which cannot visit a person who has inner turmoil. Are you upset? How will the grace of God come? What is better, to forgive our brother and feel the grace of God, or to have turmoil? We should say, "They are human. The evil one tempted them to say a few words; they weren't themselves."

August 20th

Of course we should ask forgiveness before the sun sets so that we can sleep with a clear conscience and so that our prayer is pleasing before God.

August 21st

May Christ forgive us for whatever has happened from weaknesses, passions, and faults, and grant us repentance, illumination, and sanctity in our souls, as He is a compassionate and loving God.

August 22nd

We should say what Fr. Apostolos from Kanala said: "Gerondissa, we must cling to the fringe of the Panagia's garment." We will cling to the fringe of Her garment and go to Paradise.

August 23rd

Let us continually keep our thoughts on spiritual theoria, at times embracing the feet of Christ, and at other times embracing His Cross where His All-Holy blood was shed to cleanse us. After Christ, we should go to the Panagia. We should embrace Her little feet, look into Her sweet eyes, and speak to Her noetically. We should have Her as a mediator, because our prayer has no boldness and we are not worthy to call on the name of Christ.

August 24th

How beautifully he [St. John the Theologian] says, "In the beginning was the Word, and the Word was with God, and the word was God." What a great mystery this is! We should have great reverence for him [St. John] and ask him to grant us love.

August 25th

We will fight with the evil one! He will come into our mind and suggest one thing or another. If we do not expel and cast out those rotten, filthy things from our mind, we will not find help. Everyone battles hard. Who does not have warfare? Even the saints of the desert who reached God had struggles.

August 26th

Work should be done with prudence and the fear of God. When we do our handiwork, we should not talk idly but should say the prayer, "Lord Jesus Christ, have mercy on me," and "Most Holy Theotokos, save us."

August 27th

One Holy Father said, just as we approach Holy Communion with fear and trembling, in the same manner we should have reverence for our brethren because they are the image of God. If we treat every person in this way, it is impossible that God will not forgive us, because God is love.

August 28th

Whoever works more will profit more. Whoever works very little and avoids a job because it is difficult will not have gifts or wages. I am telling you this because through toil and labor I came to know Christ.

August 29th

God bestows grace on a person and sanctifies him. What more did the Holy Fathers have? They were people with passions and weaknesses, too. They fought against all the passions, but since they had good intentions and struggled, they attained holiness.

August 30th

In the church, it is said that there are more holy angels present than the number of our breaths. Just think what happens in church during the time of the Holy Eucharist. This is why a person should remain still, noetically kneeling at the feet of Christ and the Panagia, and saying the words of the prayer with great attention and feeling: "Lord Jesus Christ, have mercy on me." In this way, one experiences spiritual states.

August 31st

Many times we promise God that we will be His children and make a good beginning, but the devil comes and throws us into one temptation or another, and we fall. Saint Nikodemos of the Holy Mountain says we need to make a good beginning every day.

September

September 1st

When I was working in the world and would finish before the other women, I did not feel right to be without work. I would help them in order for us to finish all together. We were content with each other and had mutual harmony, love, and support.

September 2nd

Let us persistently knock on the door, and the Lord will open to us because He loves us. He loves us so much! We have a Father Who is all affection, all love.

September 3rd

The grace of God that comes with the sweetest name of Jesus softens the soul. The world could be upside down, yet inside a person there is meekness, self-control, peace, and a spiritual state of great delight.

September 4th

When someone… struggles in trying to cast off his passions, he sees God within his soul, and he continually feels that he is living in a corner of Paradise.

September 5th

When we begin any task, we should think that God is watching us and that our guardian angel is with us. Therefore, anything we do should be done with piety and faith, and then every endeavor will have the blessing of God.

September 6th

The compassion of God is endless like the ocean, like the heavens. God does not say, "Why did you fall?" but instead, "Why didn't you get up?"

September 7th

Sister Vrieni would say, "I do not have words to thank my big brother [guardian angel], who stands next to me when I work and when I pray and is constantly laboring for me. Shouldn't I also strive not to sadden him?"

September 8th

The saints have us in their care. They feel pain and suffer along with us. They constantly run to help us, even if our eyes are closed and we do not see them.

September 9th

We cannot deceive the eye of God, which sees everything - our movements, our thoughts, everything.

September 10th

Now, let us reflect a little on Hell, which we do not keep in our minds at all. If we keep Hell in our minds, we will be very careful about falsely accusing or insinuating. Did we hear something? We should say, "Hey, wait, maybe I did not hear well. Maybe that is not correct...

September 11th

Then the elder [Geronda Ieronymos] said to us, "Look here. When you walk, you should see people like trees. When I walk, I see the people like trees, and my thoughts are pure; they are not stained in any way. Always use the back roads, not the main ones; follow the narrow and afflicted way."

September 12th

We must understand very well that when we see someone else's fall, we should think of our own fall. We are in the same boat, "bearing flesh and living in the world", because our flesh is all passions and shortcomings.

September 13th

What spiritual unity takes place when one communicates with another! This is how the grace of God is transmitted! One person has grace and he gives it to another. What grandeur!

September 14th

Let us struggle, saying, "My Christ, have mercy on me, strengthen me, give me zeal to love and worship you.

September 15th

Even if just a little at a time, we must struggle for our salvation. Even if we ascend only as much as the width of the tip of a needle, we must still ascend little by little and not descend. When a thought comes to us, we must immediately be vigilant and watchful! We have so many wonderful books, so many homilies, and so many beautiful things available that open our minds every day.

September 16th

…may the Archangel Michael take us at a good hour. We don't know in what state he will find us at the hour of death. May Christ give us zeal and diligence to do whatever we haven't done up until now - first of all myself, because I don't have what I should to offer to our Christ.

September 17th

We must be careful not to judge - extremely careful! It is so terrible that it is beyond words! "Judge not, that ye be not judged." Have we kept this? Even if we have no virtue but we don't judge, Christ will save us and take us to Paradise.

September 18th

We have our guardian angel right beside us; we should love him very much! We should honor him and thank him! We must give him joy with our deeds, our love, our behavior, and the way we live!

September 19th

As someone has said, there are more holy angels than the breaths we take. Just imagine!

September 20th

Our nous should be in Heaven. Sometimes we should take it to the throne of Christ, sometimes to the Panagia's throne, and sometimes to the beauty of Paradise. If we become enthusiastic about some lovely thing here, just think about how it will be in Heaven!

We should occupy our mind with these things so that the devil does not encircle us with trivial things...

September 21st

If we have much love for Christ, everything will be easy. Our mind will be filled with light and our soul full of delight.

September 22nd

Sorrow and temptations precedes, and then comes grace and consolation.

September 23rd

When you whisper the name of God and are careful in everything, you will see what grandeur you will feel. The nous will have light and the soul will have great blessings.

September 24th

First we should think, and then we should express what we want to say, logically, calmly, kindly, and with meekness and love of God.

September 25th

It is not that we are unable, but we are unwilling to struggle.

September 26th

As the grace of God visits a person's soul, the person seeks to experience different spiritual states, and he entreats the saints that he may be made worthy to be a participant with them.

September 27th

In our prayers, we should entreat God saying, "Lord Jesus Christ, heal Your servants who are in the hospitals; help Your servants who are imprisoned; enlighten the sinners." Thus a prisoner will be illumined, a sinner will be saved. You ask, "How did that person come to repentance? How did that happen?" It is from the prayers of the faithful.

September 28th

Bitterness is from the devil, and the cross that God gives us to bear is lifted by His grace. We must immerse our nous in the Holy Spirit, in the Nous of God, and then we will see His majesty.

September 29th

Do you want to be deprived of seeing all the lovely flowers that are all alike [in Heaven]?

They do not differ in the least, and when they wave in the breeze, the fluttering they make pours out an inexpressible fragrance.

September 30th

Be very careful when someone approaches to tell you something about someone else. You should say, "Please, I don't want you to tell me about someone else. Do me this favor."

October

October 1st

When someone struggles to do what is right, God will not abandon him. He fills his treasure chest with "money." He fills it with virtues, and the person will be loaded with these as he ascends to Heaven.

October 2nd

Let us struggle so that we may enjoy the beauty of Paradise with its precious flowers that are all even in height, and its pleasant breeze that refreshes, enlivens, and brings so much delight!

October 3rd

When someone sees himself as a zero and his passions as immense, then he is approaching God. However, if instead he looks around at what others are doing, he is far from God.

October 4th

Let us pursue the prayer persistently, just like someone who hunts for a diamond. This prayer will teach us to love Christ.

October 5th

We should take our soul by the hand and take it for a walk. "Come, let me take you to Paradise to taste its splendor. I will take you to the throne of God to delight in your Bridegroom. Come, I will also take you to Hades." Do not allow your nous to wander right and left all day long like a vagabond.

Afterwards, the soul is exhausted, and it comes back tired and dirty.

October 6th

We need to discern what is from God and what is from the devil, and whatever is from the devil we need to avoid and expel from ourselves. Envy, criticism, hatred, and remembrance of wrongs - all of these are from the devil, and we must cast them out.

October 7th

We must be attentive to our thoughts, our mouth, our ears, our five senses. When we are not careful of these, then we think others are at fault. When divine grace comes, repentance and tears follow.

October 8th

Do we labor for any of the saints, so that we can make them our mediator on the Day of Judgment? For this reason, we must say with much piety, "Holy angels and all the saints, intercede for us," and venerate their icons.

October 9th

You should know that the grace of God departs because of three things: pride, egotism, and the passions of the flesh.

October 10th

All of the passions are inside us. So, you see, when we do not do our prayers regularly and we are not careful, our ego and all of the passions spring up, and we do things that are not right. ...and we will give an account to God for our deeds.

October 11th

Keep in mind that no matter what a person does, nothing remains hidden. Do not say, "I will do this secretly, and it won't be noticed." No matter what a person does, it will be revealed.

October 12th

God will judge each person, and each person has his own inner world. We judge one way, but we don't know what God will do. We take the judgment away from God. The devil tricks us, and we say, "There's no one like me. I never do this, I never do that," and yet, we do these things.

October 13th

I had a little shawl, and I wrapped it around her shoulders [the woman ascetic in the Kleisoura area of Castoria]. She was very pleased with it! "Just as you have covered me," she told me, "thus may your angel cover you, and may the Panagia keep you under Her protection."

October 14th

When there is no fear of God in our soul, we are like the unburied dead. Is the fear of God missing? Everything is missing. There is no heavenly grandeur, harmony, love, illumination, or sanctity. The gifts of the Holy Spirit are "love, joy, peace, longsuffering, kindness, goodness, faith, meekness, abstinence..."

October 15th

Just as we try to make time to do something that we want, and we manage to find time, likewise we must find time to do what God wants. We will find time for prayer, for the services...

October 16th

Joy is not talking and conversing with one person or another; only Christ gives joy. He gives unspeakable joy that one cannot imagine, a secret joy that cannot be expressed. This kind of joy is received in a person's soul, and he says, "O, that I had wings as a dove, then would I fly away, and be at rest. Who will give me years to work for my God?"

October 17th

What a beautiful thing it is for one to be patient!

October 18th

When you cannot sleep and various thoughts come to your mind, say the Salutations [O Theotokos and Virgin rejoice...] continually, and sleep will come and the Panagia will give you much joy.

October 19th

When you love God immensely and have Him in your heart, your soul is refined with a certain nobility that teaches you how to behave, how to speak, and in general how to improve your spiritual demeanor. Christ becomes the Teacher, the Professor, the Rector of the soul, and teaches the person such beautiful things, as though he had gone to a university.

October 20th

This is how we should love our neighbor, so much that we sacrifice ourselves. When we see someone struggling with a difficult task, we should go and help, no matter how tired we may be.

October 21st

We must live with watchfulness. Christ says, "Watch and pray, that ye enter not into temptation." "Pray without ceasing, in everything give thanks." This means that the mind must be vigilant.

October 22nd

Our passions should not conquer us. We all have passions and shortcomings. As soon as a passion sprouts up, we must immediately uproot it so that it does not grow deep roots and later cannot be uprooted.

October 23rd

If we want to help ourselves, we must see only our own faults and continually take our mind to the throne of God. We should take our mind to the throne of Christ and from there to the throne of the Panagia, saying sweet words to our Lady Theotokos and thanking Her for bearing with us...

October 24th

Christ did not laugh in His earthly life; He only wept because He was thinking about our salvation. He saw that He would carry the Cross and suffer an unjust martyrdom. There would be many who would not believe in Him: "Many are called, but few are chosen." Christ had sorrow and great pain because He was thinking how His Crucifixion would not redeem the whole human race.

October 25th

Oh, what is prepared for us in the Jerusalem on high! For this reason, the Fathers were captivated by prayer and abandoned family and all glory and luxury. They put on poor shepherd's clothing and went to the monastery, pretending to be uneducated and illiterate peasants, just so they would be assigned the lowliest possible tasks.

October 26th

When we are saying the prayer, even if we do not understand it, it is working within us and protects us in temptations, and at the same time it will help another sister who has a temptation.

October 27th

Be attentive to yourselves as much as possible. Every night, we should take account of our sins. We should say, "Whom did I sadden? Whom did I speak badly about? What did I disregard?" We do not want to have a guilty conscience.

October 28th

I say to Her ...You are the Mother of God, and I desire for You to help us. I want to see all of these souls in Paradise, whether we are worthy to be saved or not."

October 29th

A person must strive to put his thoughts in correct order, so that he does not allow himself to stray away from the grandeur of God's Divinity. He should say to himself, "Listen, God Himself was crucified, scourged, slapped and spit upon. He suffered. Who am I? And if someone offends me, so what? It doesn't matter.

October 30th

Some angels have six wings, and they cover their faces with their wings due to the brilliant Light of God; they cannot endure to look upon His Divinity! What an amazing thing! Our minds cannot even begin to fathom this.

October 31st

We should fervently love our guardian angel who stands beside us, censer in hand, listening to us as he censes us with incense. That is why wherever the Fathers went, they felt the fragrance of their angel.

November

November 1st

There is need for humility in our souls. Through humility, we will be saved, and God will bestow on us abundant grace.

November 2nd

For every effort we put forth, God will reward us. He leaves no one unrewarded and pays us all generously. However, we do not see this now; we will see it in Paradise.

November 3rd

We must entreat Christ to grant us patience. When we go to our work, we should cross ourselves and say, "My Christ, strengthen me that I may pass through this day without grieving You and that I may sing hymns to You."

November 4th

When we give our love to Christ, He will give us all His love in return.

November 5th

Courtesy is something majestic in a person and especially in a spiritual person. We should not speak harshly, for harshness impedes the grace of God. Let us make use of our time, for we will long to have these moments back, but we will not find them again.

November 6th

When a person says the prayer, everything inside him is put in order, and he has peace.

November 7th

When we see that we are being attacked by a passion, let us immediately cry out, "My Christ, help me, strengthen me, this passion is battling me."

November 8th

When this light [of divine grace] comes into our soul, we should embrace it. We then see the "dust" and the "germs" in our soul.

November 9th

The holy angels cover their faces from the brilliance of the Godhead; they cannot set eyes on God's immense grandeur. ...the resplendence of God's face permeates all of Paradise.

November 10th

As much as possible, we need to strive to reach God, because in the future we will seek these days that are passing but we will not find them again. We should speak with love and kindness.

November 11th

...to cook a meal we stand on our feet for hours until it is done. Are we not laboring? Don't we become tired?

Doesn't it take a half hour, forty-five minutes to eat? And don't all these things occupy us? Yes, we willingly do all this work. Likewise, at the time of prayer we should compel ourselves saying that we need to do our prayers.... And you will see how the grace of God will come into the soul.

November 12th

If you take up the sword, you will die by the sword. If you do good, you will find good; if you do evil, you will find evil. God illumines, and everything is discovered.

November 13th

Even great saints have fallen. So we should be watchful and accept whatever God allows. We must fall down before the throne of God and of the Panagia. When we work on all these things, divine grace will strengthen us and remove everything evil inside us....

November 14th

...just as we are attentive in church, so we must be attentive during trapeza as well.

November 15th

When the spirit of grace is in our soul, we will be careful how we speak. We will be careful not to be bold, wrathful, angry, or judgmental. All these things separate us from God. You know what it says in the Gospel, "Judge not that ye be not judged." Judging is the greatest sin and the most terrible of the seven deadly sins.

November 16th

What did St. Anthony the Great say? Without temptations, no one can be saved - no one at all.

November 17th

[Gerondissa quoting a homily,] "Take the Panagia into your arms, into your embrace, and entreat Her to help you, to forgive you, and to ignite the divine fire in your soul." We stand fast through the intercessions of our Panagia.

November 18th

Let us take our salvation very seriously.

November 19th

When divine grace overshadows a person's soul, the tears begin to stream effortlessly, and he says, "What is this? What beauty is this, what delight! My Christ, take me now to Paradise that I may behold You! Tears come from the remembrance of death, when one contemplates his mortality and corrects himself.

November 20th

...we should have much respect and live like the angels. Does an angel get angry? Does an angel argue? Does an angel debate, lie, judge... Never!

November 21st

The grace of the Panagia is one, the grace of Christ is another, the saints have another, the Cross has another, and the Holy Trinity yet another. When we supplicate and beseech them, we perceive their grace.

November 22nd

No matter how much vivacity the body has, the refinement of Christ's teaching which comes to the soul humbles a person. It makes him an earthly angel with graceful speech and movements, able to bear with everything. We must forbear so that God will also bear with us.

November 23rd

All day long we should try to encourage, assist, and lift up our neighbor. If a person labors spiritually like this every day, he will endure the injustices that he encounters for the love of his neighbor with a thankful and grateful attitude.

November 24th

[Our Lady Theotokos] covers us with Her vast protection and entreats Her Son for us all, saying, "My Lord, My sweetest Son and God, save Your creation. Help them and grant them Your grace...." Our Panagia's immeasurable love cannot be comprehended!

November 25th

In our minds we must grasp the reality that our death means facing God's Judgment. Where will we go, where will we end up - in Hades or in Paradise?

November 26th

Our discussions should be with great humility, not with raised voices. Explain everything nicely and calmly. Wherever there is humility, there is the grace of God.

November 27th

Indeed, do we truly believe in Christ? Do we truly love Christ? Where is our love? Do we love Him and adore Him with all our heart, with all our soul, and with all our mind?

November 28th

Once, when Geronda Joseph underwent a great temptation, he went into the desert to pray, and as he was crying out to God, he saw a vision of a large, beautiful bird singing. In a moment, he found himself in Paradise where there were many birds. The birds were angels, and among them was the large bird, singing and keeping the bass note. Imagine that! He saw it with his own eyes!

November 29th

Let us do the will of God. Let us feel the compassion of God, Who waits for us with His open embrace.

November 30th

When someone does not pay attention to details, takes things superficially, and strays here and there indifferently, he ends up saying, "What does it matter?" This is a fall. Later, we will say, "How did this darkness come over me? How is it that I have no appetite for prayer and these thoughts are choking me?"

December

December 1st

Through saying the prayer, a person feels divine consolation and heavenly grandeur. …when we grumble and talk idly, God leaves, and we occupy ourselves with the faults of others.

December 2nd

When a person has the prayer, he does not express himself with shouting, gestures, or grimaces. The grace of God at work in his soul makes him meek, humble, and gentle. However, because we forget to say the prayer, we get angry and argue.

December 3rd

Whatever prayer a person utters, whatever spiritual struggle he undertakes, whatever he abstains from - noetically, physically, or spiritually - whatever he has saved to the side, if it is all done as labor for God, it is written and remains in His book. God sees our every struggle, and the guardian angel of our soul records them all, while the devil takes his own notes.

December 4th

Prayer requires earnest pursuit. If we do this, even when we fall we will immediately realize our mistake, and we will repent.

December 5th

Prayer does not mean doing your rule on your prayer rope hastily, with your mind wandering. Prayer means saying words to Christ, beseeching Him to help you be saved. Then you feel Christ responding to you and speaking to you very sweetly with such tenderness, just as a father speaks to his child.

December 6th

He forgives us for everything; it is enough that we repent as soon as we understand we have made a mistake.

December 7th

There were other Holy Fathers who went to Mount Athos, like Saint John Koukouzelis, who would chant when he took the goats out to graze, and the goats would stand up on their hind legs in praise to God. The Fathers were glorified both in Heaven and on earth because of their great humility.

December 8th

When we chase after the prayer, divine grace protects us. It comes like the dew which enlivens the grass. Likewise it soaks into the roots of our heart and revives us.

December 9th

Whenever our guardian angel wakes us, we should begin to pray at that very moment; let us not allow ourselves any slack. When our though tells us to sleep a little more, we should not sleep.

December 10th

Our work should be accompanied by prayer. When one wants to find God, he will also find Him while working.

December 11th

Whatever one does for the love of Christ, he will find again later in his life. If someone works for an employer an hour or two more than required, he will be paid even more for the overtime. How much more with God, Who repays us for every labor we do for His sake.

December 12th

...covered with ash and barefoot like a fool for Christ.... That elder's charity was beyond words. You can't imagine how much charity he had. He would walk down the road, and when he saw a poor person he gave him his shoes and came home barefoot, or he took off his raso and gave it away, coming home in his cassock.

December 13th

Be attentive in church.... At that moment, you are noetically at the throne of God, hymning God like the angels. So, just as the holy angels stand with fear, you should try to imitate them.

December 14th

...a monk who was negligent... didn't do his monastic duties, but he didn't judge anyone either. He became seriously ill and was very serene, waiting peacefully for his death. His brothers came to comfort him. "What have you done, brother, that makes you so calm?" the elder asked him. "I have done nothing up to this day, only that I didn't judge anyone... When he died, the holy angels came to take him to Heaven.

December 15th

Let us not lose time. Our days and years are passing by, so we should not let the devil steal away our time. Has a day passed? It is gone. It is wrapped up, and the angel goes and deposits our good works while the demons collect our bad works.

December 16th

We must force ourselves.... Our body is like a horse: it wants to sleep, eat, be looked after, and live an easy life. It gets weary of doing one thing or another and slacks off, lacking the willingness for either spiritual or physical labor. For this reason, we must strive to do the will of God, to love Christ and the Panagia exceedingly.

December 17th

…when one approaches God, one sees his angel by his side, accompanying him; he sees the saints next to him, hymning, singing, and glorifying God. This is the secret joy in the soul of man, not found in a worldly or easy life or in sleep or in various mundane things.

December 18th

Let us draw closer to God, to perceive Him, to taste Him, to have Him in our hearts, to worship Him. Christ must be inside us and no one else.

December 19th

You should pray to the All-Holy Trinity on your prayer ropes, saying, "O Holy Trinity, our God, have mercy on us," because the Holy Trinity imparts grace to a person and he becomes a dwelling place of the Holy Spirit. The soul becomes like a shining dove. The Holy Spirit comes and illumines and brings warmth, refreshing a person's heart and burning up like a fire whatever passions and shortcomings he has.

December 20th

The grace of God is so overwhelming! How good God is! He forbears, forbears, and forbears! ...The earth cries out, "I cannot endure mankind any longer. I cannot bear the sin any longer." And God answers, "Patience. Just as I forgive, you must also forbear."

December 21st

I have seen God in toil. When a person avoids labor, avoids difficulties, saying, "Oh, I can't go there," and "Oh, I can't do that," he becomes selfish and protects himself.... We will struggle for the love of God. If one does not struggle, he is not crowned.

December 22nd

Negligence is the greatest deadly sin because from negligence comes slothfulness, and slothfulness gives birth to forgetfulness and the darkening of the nous. When a person has the grace of God, he does the will of God, and through labor in prayer he flies with new wings and his soul is transformed.

December 23rd

We do not pay attention to the law of God and how we should act, but to what others tell us, and we do whatever they do. They might lose their souls. Should

I lose mine, too? Instead, I am going to focus on what the Gospel of Christ says so I can make progress.

December 24th

God has given us so many beautiful things, and if we were to sense them in our soul, we would have so much joy that we would fly, we would flutter into Christ's embrace.

December 25th

A spiritual person will experience Paradise here on earth and in Heaven...."Be ye holy, for I am holy. Christ is "a jealous God...." He does not want our heart to be divided, to be scattered here and there, but to be given over entirely to Him.

December 26th

What a powerful thing! Man cannot comprehend it; he is overcome by awe. That is what happens when one reflects on how man becomes a god by grace and how anyone becomes worthy to speak with God if only he approaches Him. Divine consolation then visits a person's soul, and he sees Christ, the Panagia, and the saints. He sees them next to him, like brothers, like relatives.

December 27th

One time, Mr. Panagopoulos came and told me, "I know someone who felt the fluttering wings of his guardian angel." I answered, "Mr. Panagopoulos, it must have been you." He lowered his head without speaking.

December 28th

In order to have great faith in God we must entrust Him to "increase our faith," because faith and love are gifts of God. If we do not call upon the name of God and do not implore Him, He does not give us these gifts.

December 29th

You don't know how much boldness a person receives when he prays for another. You can't imagine what grace one receives when one prays for someone who saddened him. I remember my father, who said, "My child, for the worst thing that somebody does to you, you will in turn do the best for him. Show your love to everyone, and God will repay you abundantly." I was a small child then, and I remember everything he told us. He said, "Love my little child!" and I imprinted it firmly in my mind.

December 30th

Yet another year has passed. Blessed is the one who made a good beginning and struggled, who stored up spiritual provisions, did the will of God, and walked well-pleasing to God.

December 31st

This is what I ask for in my humble prayers, saying, "All-Holy Trinity, illumine them, watch over them, and send down Your Holy Spirit to give them the spirit of knowledge and truth, so that they can feel You within them and experience the spiritual life."

This book is dedicated to:

The Greek Monastery of St. John the Forerunner in Goldendale, Washington, especially Gerondissa Efpraxia who has helped me through most of my adult life.

Sean Fitzgerald, Martha Courtney, Wayne Ruckman, and Jana Hallford, who carried me through my 2020 coronavirus experience.

You. I hope you love and are helped in your spiritual journey by the treasure of Gerondissa Makrina's spiritual wisdom.

Acknowledgements:

Cover Photo: Wolfgang Hasselmann via Unsplash

Cover Design: Danisha Asif

Printed in Dunstable, United Kingdom